P9-CAR-551

THE SCIENCE OF OPTICAL ILLUSIONS

PUZZLING PICTURES

Gareth Stevens
PUBLISHING

ANNA CLAYBOURNE

Please visit our website, **www.garethstevens.com**.
For a free color catalog of all our high-quality books,
call toll free 1-800-542-2595 or fax 1-877-542-2596.

Cataloging-in-Publication Data
Names: Claybourne, Anna.
Title: Puzzling pictures / Anna Claybourne.
Description: New York : Gareth Stevens Publishing, 2020. | Series: The science of optical illusions | Includes glossary and index.
Identifiers: ISBN 9781538242452 (pbk.) | ISBN 9781538241875 (library bound) | ISBN 9781538242469 (6 pack)
Subjects: LCSH: Optical illusions--Juvenile literature. | Visual perception--Juvenile literature.
Classification: LCC QP495.C5725 2020 | DDC 152.14'8--dc23

First Edition

Published in 2020 by
Gareth Stevens Publishing
111 East 14th Street, Suite 349
New York, NY 10003

Photo credits: p8 © Kiev.Victor; p9 t Salvador Dali / Alamy Stock Photo, b Public Domain; p10 Richard Gregory; p11 t Glasshouse Images / Alamy Stock Photo, b Mat Edwards; p13 t DAVID MACK, b Raticova; p14 © István Orosz; p15 t vexworldwide, b Iryna Kuznetsova; p17 b Mat Edwards; p18 Nick Higham / Alamy Stock Photo; p19 Vladimir Sazonov; p23 Creative Commons; p24 t Michael Doolittle / Alamy Stock Photo, b Mat Edwards; p25 b Alamy Stock Photo; p26 Hans Holbein / Public Domain; p27 t Creative Commons, b Mat Edwards; p29 b Mat Edwards

Printed in the United States of America

CPSIA compliance information: Batch #CS19GS: For further information contact Gareth Stevens, New York, New York at 1-800-542-2595.

CONTENTS

INTRODUCTION

WHAT ARE OPTICAL ILLUSIONS?

The word "optical" has to do with light and how we see it. An illusion is something that tricks you, so that you don't experience it as it really is.

Magicians and illusionists make impossible things appear to happen. This performer can't really make this die levitate—but he makes it look as if he can.

SEEING IS BELIEVING

When we look around and see things, it feels to us as if we're simply seeing the world as it really is. However, that's not quite true. Your eyes and your brain can make mistakes, miss things, or even see things that aren't there. An optical illusion is a picture that takes advantage of these mistakes to play a trick on you.

HOW HUMANS SEE

1. Light rays from objects enter the eye.

2. Light hits the retina at the back of the eyeball.

3. Light-sensitive cells in the retina detect patterns of light.

4. The cells send signals to the brain along the optic nerve.

5. The brain interprets the signals to figure out what they mean.

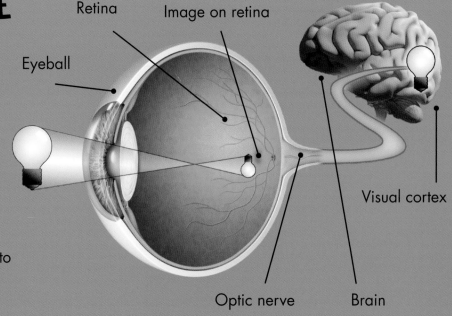

Retina   Image on retina

Eyeball

Visual cortex

Optic nerve   Brain

TOO MUCH INFORMATION!

All day long, there's a constant flood of images entering your eyes and zooming into your brain. There's so much information, your brain simply can't process it all carefully.

Instead, it decides what it's looking at by matching the light patterns it sees to its memories and previous experiences. It ignores or shuts out things that don't seem important and will quickly jump to conclusions to save time.

Here's an example. What can you see in this picture? ▶

Most people would see two friends riding these. ▼

In other words, bicycles—machines with two round wheels of equal size. But you only "see" that because of your brain's knowledge and experience. The wheels you actually saw look like this:

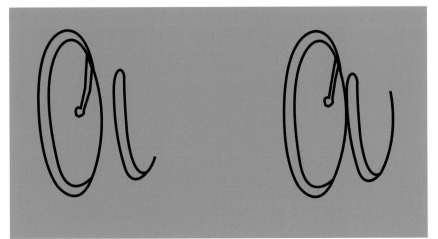

ILLUSIONS GALORE

This book is packed with incredible optical illusions to bamboozle your brain—from impossible objects to pictures that can be seen in more than one way. Turn the page to get started!

TWO VIEWS

What's this a picture of? Do you see a tall vase? Look at the spaces on either side of it—do they look like anything familiar?

This type of illusion is called Rubin's vase. The vase is shaped so that, although it looks fairly normal, the spaces on either side of it look like two faces in profile.

Most people find it hard to see both of these images at once. You can look at the vase, or you can "flip" your brain and look at the faces.

How Does It Work?

This illusion was invented in 1915 by Edgar Rubin, a psychologist (someone who studies the mind). He found that when the brain sees shapes, it quickly figures out which part is the "object" it's looking at and which part is the "background."

A Rubin's vase illusion confuses the brain by making the background also seem like a recognizable object. The brain doesn't handle that very well, since it likes to make quick decisions about what it can see.

The Rubin's vase illusion

DUCK OR RABBIT?

Here's another famous double-vision illusion. You can see this as a duck with its beak sticking out to the left—or as a rabbit facing right with its ears behind it.

Which is it? It keeps changing! As with the vase, you can focus on seeing the duck or seeing the rabbit. Your brain doesn't want to do both at the same time.

There are lots of different versions of this illusion. You could even try drawing your own!

The famous duck-rabbit illusion

OLD AND YOUNG

Here's one more to try. Do you see a young woman wearing a dark necklace turning away from you? Or do you see a big-nosed older woman with a long chin, looking forward?

ILLUSION ART

Artists sometimes like to use trick double images in their work.

The Face of Mae West, an illusion in a room

One artist who especially loved optical illusions was the Spanish surrealist painter and sculptor Salvador Dalí.

Check out this room made by Dalí, called *The Face of Mae West.* Mae West was a movie star and writer who was famous for her glamorous looks. Dalí set up the room with paintings, curtains, and a strangely shaped sofa, so that as you enter the room, you see the star's face.

WHO'S IN THE MARKET?

Here's another Dalí creation: a painting called *Slave Market with the Disappearing Bust of Voltaire*. It's a picture of women walking through an archway—but the shapes in the picture also make up an image of the French philosopher Voltaire.

WE'RE ALL DOOMED!

Throughout history, artists and writers have liked to point out that no matter how much money you have or how fancy you look, in the end, everyone will get old, die, and be left as a pile of bones.

This picture by American illustrator Charles Allan Gilbert is a classic example—it's called *All Is Vanity*. A beautifully dressed lady sits at her table full of makeup and perfume, admiring her reflection. She looks as if she's about to go to a fabulous party.

But take a step back, and—yikes! All the details in the picture make up the shape of an enormous spooky skull!

Brain-Boggling!

The skull picture is very effective because the two different ways of seeing the painting put you in very different moods. When you see the skull, it makes you jump!

HIDDEN ANIMALS

Can you find the animals hiding in these pictures?

SPOT THE DOG

It may look like a pattern of random blobs and dots, but there's a spotty Dalmatian dog hiding somewhere in this spot-covered picture. If you can't find it, it's very frustrating! But once you do see it, it's impossible not to see it.

The spotted hidden Dalmatian illusion

How Does It Work?

To locate and identify objects in its field of vision, your brain looks for edges. Edges tell us the shape of an object and help us to separate it from its background. If you're looking at a spotted animal on a spotted background, you just get a general impression of spots, and the edges are really hard to see.

Once you do see the dog, though, your brain matches its shape to the records of "dog shapes" stored in your memory. This helps it "fix" the image of the dog, so that it doesn't lose it again.

Brain-Boggling!

Many animals have patterns that help them to hide by breaking up their outline and making it hard to see their shape. Tiger and zebra stripes, for example, break up the animal's outline when it's standing in long grass.

The Puzzled Fox by Currier & Ives

THE PUZZLED FOX

Never mind one spotted dog ... this old illustration has 15 animals and human faces in it, not counting the fox! Some are obvious, but some are more hidden. To find them, look carefully at the patterns in the tree trunks and plants. Also look at the shapes of the spaces between things.

NIGHT IN THE FOREST

There's another, very large wild animal hiding in this picture of a forest under a night sky.

Is it lurking in the shadows or behind the trees? When you do see it, it becomes totally obvious.

IN AND OUT

These illusions can be seen in two different ways: sticking out and pointing inward.

This is a pretty simple drawing; yet, you can probably see it in two different ways. Are you looking slightly downward onto a cube on a flat surface—or looking up at the underside of a cube floating in midair?

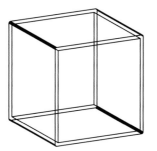

The same thing happens with the picture below. Which corners of the cubes are sticking out toward you—the corners at the bottom of the red diamonds or the corners at the tops of the diamonds?

Necker cubes

How Does It Work?

These pictures, called Necker cubes, show how the brain interprets lines and shapes as 3-D objects. The first "cube" is just a set of lines, and the "cube" pattern is just a combination of colored shapes. But your brain is used to a 3-D world, so it always sees things as 3-D shapes if it can. There are two ways these pictures could show cubes, so both of them are options for your brain.

Brain-Boggling!

Some robots can "see" using cameras and computer software. Scientists often show them Necker cubes to test how good they are at identifying things.

HOLLOW FACE

Your brain's need to see in 3-D especially applies to faces. The photo here shows a hollowed-out face, like the impression you would get if you pressed your face into soft clay. But when you look at it—even in real life—you can't help seeing a real-looking, 3-D face sticking out toward you!

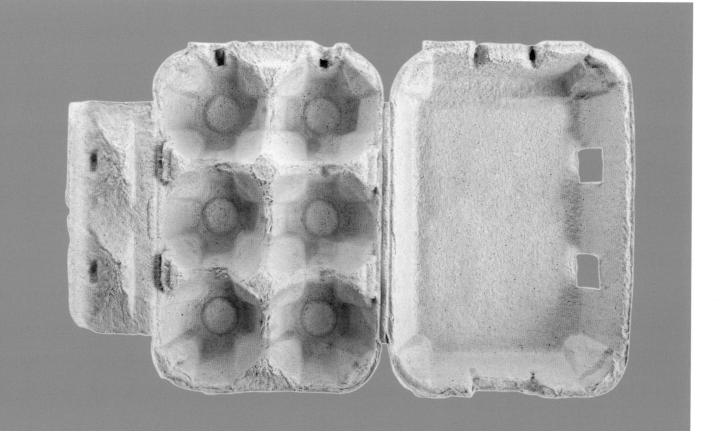

EGG CARTON EXPERIMENT

Try this weird in-and-out experiment. Here's a photo of a small egg carton that has little hollows in it. Sit next to a lamp or a bright window and slowly spin this book around. As the light seems to hit different sides of the egg carton, you might find that the hollows appear to change into peaks!

STRANGE STAIRS

Like a Necker cube, stairs can look a little confusing if you don't have enough clues about which way up they are—or if you have clues that don't seem to match up, as in this strange illusion!

How Does It Work?

Stairs are a little bit like cubes—but even simpler! When you look at stairs, all you have is a row of lines. You need other clues to tell you which parts are the steps you can stand on and which parts are the vertical edges. In the image above, Hungarian artist István Orosz has combined two different perspectives to achieve this impossible staircase.

Luckily, when we're on a real flight of stairs, we get plenty of clues—from light and shadows, the surroundings, and our sense of gravity and touch. And your brain learns how to make sense of them early in life. Otherwise, people would fall down the stairs a lot more than they do!

STAIR NIGHTMARE!

This room contains a *lot* of stairs. You might find yourself asking, "Which way is up?" Artworks like this are often called "Escheresque," after the Dutch artist M. C. Escher, who was fascinated by impossible architecture. ▶

AROUND AND AROUND!

Meanwhile, in this mind-boggling Escheresque picture, the stairs are connected in an endless loop. Depending on which way you walked, you'd be trudging upstairs or downstairs forever. Of course, this can't happen, since the top of a flight of stairs is higher than the bottom. Escheresque art uses perspective, the way the picture moves "back" into the distance, to make the stairs seem to climb and fall.

THE UNBELIEVABLE BLIVET

These strange objects, or blivets, couldn't really exist!

At a first, very quick glance, you might think there's nothing that odd about this object. Take a closer look, though, and you'll find that it's an object that is totally impossible! It's called a blivet, also known as an "impossible fork."

How Does It Work?

A blivet has a row of sticks, legs, or other long, thin parts. But instead of staying the same all the way along, the outer edges at one end become the inner edges at the other end. Run your finger along a "prong" of one of the blivets here, and you'll see what happens.

Blivets became popular when they appeared in magazines in the 1960s, but no one knows where the idea first came from.

The basic blivet

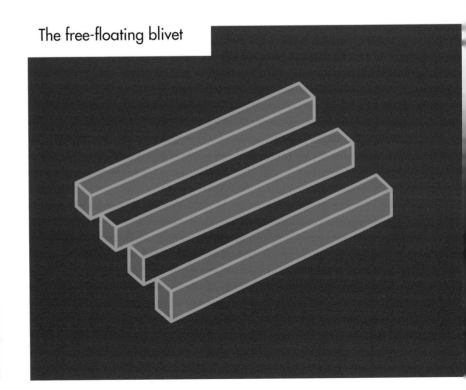

The free-floating blivet

ELEPHANT LEGS

Is this a normal elephant? No, it's a bliv-elephant. Start at the body, and like most elephants, it seems to have four legs and a trunk. Start at the feet, and something strange happens—it has five legs!

The impossible elephant illusion

I DON'T BLIVET!

Some people say the word "blivet" comes from the phrase "I don't believe it!" But actually, this word has existed for a very long time. It means any kind of small, useless object, or something that's gone wrong and is kind of a mess!

CREATE A BLIVET

Try drawing your own blivet object. There are all kinds of things it could be, such as an animal, a stool, pillars on a building, or trees. Start by drawing one end of the object, then use the space between the lines at the other end.

AMAZING ARCHITECTURE

Sometimes you can spot an optical illusion on a city street!

The almost-invisible Cira Centre

When you see an amazing optical illusion, it is usually in a book or on a computer screen—meaning it's not all that big. So imagine an optical illusion the size of an entire building! There are now quite a few of these around the world—and they can often be an astonishing sight. This one, called the Cira Centre, is a modern office building located in downtown Philadelphia, Pennsylvania.

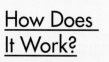

How Does It Work?

The Cira Centre achieves its amazing appearance by being totally covered in sheets of silvery glass. The people inside can see out, but the glass reflects its surroundings like a mirror.

From the right angle, when you look at the building, you see a reflection of the sky and clouds—making it seem totally see-through, or almost invisible.

18

Prague's Dancing House

DANCING HOUSE

This amazing building is in Prague, the capital of the Czech Republic. It's been designed to look as if one tower is collapsing, slumping, or melting toward the other, which leans back as if taking its weight. It gets its name because the two towers look a little like a dancing couple, one leaning in toward the other.

How Does It Work?

You'd be forgiven for not wanting to go inside, since this building does look as if it might be about to collapse. In fact, it's as strong as any building because it was designed this way. The shape of the leaning tower is made up of 99 concrete pieces; they are all different from each other and fitted together.

Brain-Boggling!

If you're wondering what the rooms inside the wonky tower must be like, you can find out! Part of the building is open to the public as a hotel.

IMPOSSIBLE SHAPES

If the cubes on page 12 seemed a little confusing, take a look at this one! Whichever way you try to see it, this square frame can't possibly exist.

IMPOSSIBLE CUBE

The picture below takes its inspiration from famous illusion-loving artist M. C. Escher, who was a fan of impossible objects. It shows an impossible-looking construction, based on the impossible cube. ▼

How Does It Work?

The impossible cube has all the parts that a normal cube has—they're just in the wrong positions.

One of the edges that should be at the back passes in front of one of the edges at the front. This could not happen in real life, unless the edges were bent and shaped in a loop—yet, they look straight.

Your brain naturally wants to see a 3-D cube. The "impossible" part means it can't work, but your brain keeps trying—resulting in confusion.

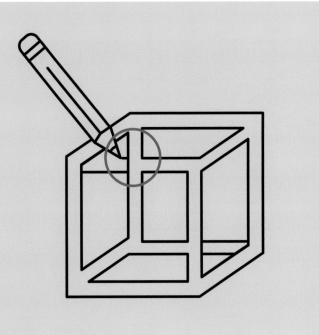

DRAW IT!

To draw an impossible cube, first draw a normal cube with a pencil. Then erase one of the edges at the front, and make the one behind it pass in front of it.

IMPOSSIBLE CIRCLE

In fact, all kinds of 3-D shapes can be drawn to break the rules of physics, like this impossible 3-D circle. While the overall outline looks right, the sides and edges don't meet up as you expect them to. Can you draw any other impossible shapes like this?

TRIANGLE TRICKS

The impossible triangle is perhaps the best-known impossible shape of all. It's known as a Penrose triangle, or sometimes a Reutersvärd triangle, after its two inventors—a scientist and an artist.

PENROSE TRIANGLE

In 1954, scientist Roger Penrose was inspired by the works of M. C. Escher to create an impossible shape. Working with his dad, Lionel Penrose, he came up with the impossible triangle. It looked something like this. ▶

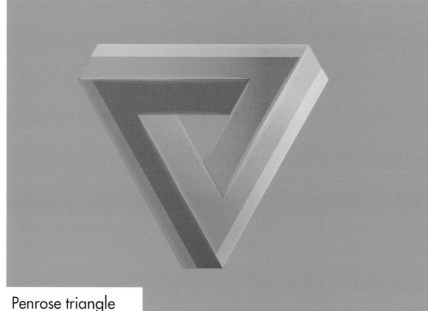

Penrose triangle

THE REUTERSVÄRD TRIANGLE

Unbeknown to the Penroses, someone had already had the same idea. Twenty years earlier, Swedish artist and designer Oscar Reutersvärd created his own impossible triangle when he was just 18. His was made up of cubes, like this. ▶

The original-style Reutersvärd triangle

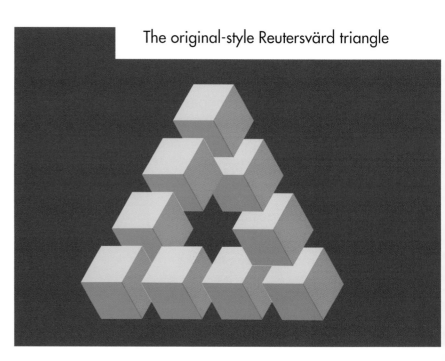

How Does It Work?

A Penrose triangle is based on a simple 3-D triangle-shaped frame, which would normally look like this:

In a Penrose triangle, the corners are different. At each corner, as you go around the triangle, each side disappears behind the next one.

That's not possible!

MAKING IT REAL

Of course, an impossible triangle can only exist in a picture, not in real life. Or can it? As this sculpture from the German Museum of Technology shows, there actually is such a thing as a real, solid impossible triangle that you can touch and feel.

How can that happen? Don't worry—it's a trick! The impossible triangle in the photo is actually not that shape at all. Below, you can see what's going on.

The object is actually shaped like this, with a gap cut in one end.

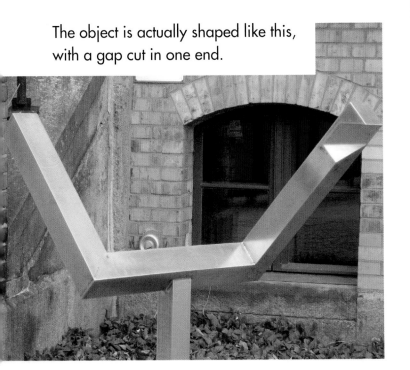

When it's seen from a particular point, the other end "fits" into the gap, making it look like a triangular object.

23

NEAR AND FAR

This is a real photo showing two people in a room. How come one of them looks like a giant?

The boy in the picture isn't really a giant. Instead, he's standing in an Ames room—a specially shaped room designed to create an amazing optical illusion.

How Does It Work?

In the photo, the Ames room looks square, but it isn't. It has a squashed, stretched shape and a tilted floor and ceiling. The boy is standing in the small corner, near the camera, where the ceiling height is very low. The woman is standing in the faraway corner, where the ceiling is higher. But seen from this exact angle, the proportions of the room look square.

Say cheese!

The boy looks bigger, but he's really just closer.

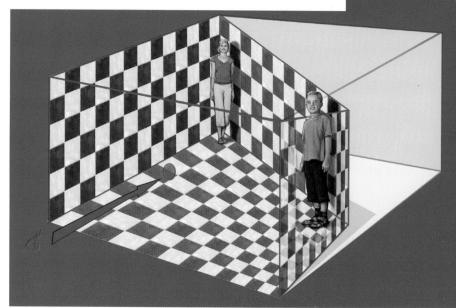

Brain-Boggling!

In fact, we see people who look extremely different in size all the time. If you're talking to a friend, and another friend appears in the distance, the first friend will be huge in comparison. Your brain ignores this, because it knows they are different distances away.

TRICK PHOTOS

You don't actually need an Ames room to use size and distance to create a very strange photo. Look at this one!

Of course, there isn't really a tiny castle sitting in a birdbath. The birdbath is just much closer. But your brain identifies objects by looking for outlines. Since the edges of the two objects line up, the brain at first assumes that it's all one thing.

DO IT YOURSELF

It's easy to take your own trick photos, especially in a big empty space such as a beach or playing field. Place an object (or person) close to the camera, and set up another object or person much farther away. Move the camera until they line up exactly.

STRETCHED IMAGES

Sometimes, all is revealed when you look at a picture in a different way.

This famous 1533 painting by Hans Holbein is called *The Ambassadors*. It shows two visitors to the court of King Henry VIII of England, who was on the throne at the time.

Most of the painting looks as old-fashioned and traditional as you'd expect. But what's that weird shape at the bottom?

You see most of the picture by looking straight at it. But to see the strange shape correctly, you have to look at it from beside and just below the painting. From that perspective, you can see that it's a skull!

How Does It Work?

This type of illusion is called anamorphosis, which means "changing shape" or "transformation." The skull is distorted in a particular way, so that it only looks normal from an extreme sideways angle.

No one is sure why Holbein did this. It might have been to show off his painting skills or as a hidden reminder that death comes to us all. Some say that he intended the picture to hang on a staircase, so that people going up the stairs would see the skull.

26

AROUND IN A CIRCLE

Another type of anamorphosis stretches the picture in a circle shape. To see it, you have to stand a special, cylinder-shaped mirror in the middle. When the stretched image is reflected, it looks like the right shape.

With the mirror in the middle, the picture is revealed.

DRAW YOUR OWN

Try drawing your own anamorphic illusion picture—it's not as hard as you might think.

- Draw a normal picture, and divide it into squares with a ruler.

- Then make a stretched grid, like the one in the picture. Copy each square onto the stretched grid, stretching the lines and shapes inside it to fit.

- Finally, trace your new, stretched picture, and try looking at it from the side.

OUT OF THE PAPER

These illusions make flat pieces of paper come to life!

Even a simple pencil drawing can become an amazing optical illusion that makes you look twice. In this example, two hands seem to come out of the paper and come to life—and each hand is busy drawing the other arm. This is yet another illustration inspired by the work of M. C. Escher—that guy was full of incredible ideas!

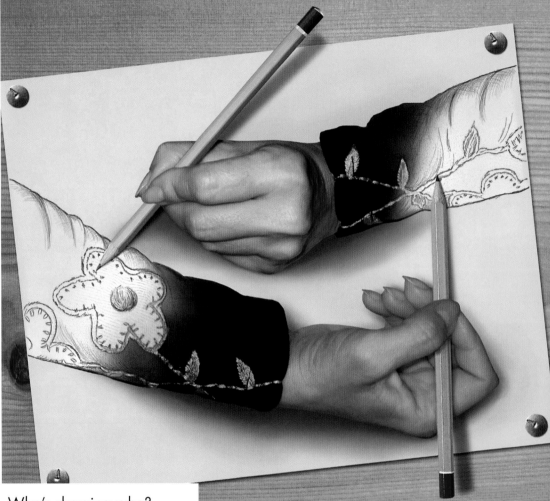

Who's drawing who?

How Does It Work?

The hands in the picture look 3-D, but the fact that they are actually drawing each other makes them seem to come to life even more. The shadows beneath the hands add the effect of them seeming to stick out, away from the paper. And the pencils are shown breaking out of a fake "piece of paper" that's really inside the picture.

AMAZING 3-D DRAWINGS

There are all kinds of ways to create pencil drawing illusions. Simple swirls can be made to look like a tunnel, as on the left, a 3-D staircase rising out of it, or a hand reaching toward you. These drawings work especially well if you see the 3-D effect from one side of the paper, which makes it look less like a flat picture. Some artists make part of the image stick out of the main rectangle of paper, too.

Brain-Boggling!

You know that it's a flat piece of paper. But your brain wants to see things in 3-D—so, as long as the trick works well enough, your brain keeps telling you it is 3-D!

DRAW YOUR OWN 3-D HAND

This is a quick and easy way to create a 3-D illusion drawing.

1. Draw closely around your hand on a plain, unlined piece of paper.

2. Add shaded-in shadows under the edge of the hand on one side.

3. Draw straight lines across the page to make it look like ruled paper, except where the hand is.

4. Connect the lines across the hand, making them curve away from you as if over the hand.

GLOSSARY

3-D Three-dimensional, which means having length, width, and depth.

anamorphosis A stretched or distorted picture that appears normal when viewed from a particular position, or using a distorted mirror or lens.

blivet A type of impossible shape with several legs, prongs, or pillars.

cells The tiny units that make up living things. Light-detecting cells are found in the retina.

field of vision The area of the outside world that a person can see as they look in a particular direction.

illusion An image that confuses the viewer and makes them see something that is different from reality.

optical To do with light, and the way our eyes detect it.

optic nerve A bundle of nerve fibers connecting the light-sensing cells in the retina to the part of the brain that makes sense of images.

perspective The way three-dimensional objects or scenes can be shown on a flat surface or understood by the brain from the shapes and patterns we see in real life.

retina An area of light-detecting cells at the back of the eyeball that sense patterns of light entering the eye.

vertical Stretching straight up and down, at right angles to the horizon.

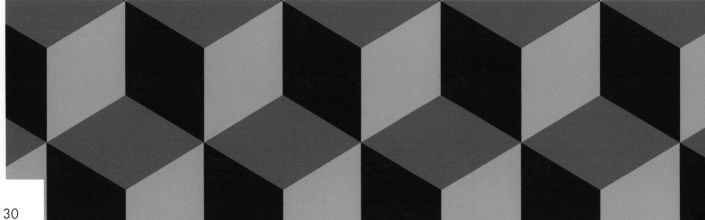

FURTHER INFORMATION

BOOKS

Gifford, Clive. *Brain Twisters: The Science of Thinking and Feeling.* Brighton, UK: Ivy Press, 2015.

Hanson, Anders, and Elissa Mann. *Cool Optical Illusions: Creative Activities That Make Math & Science Fun for Kids!* Minneapolis, MN: ABDO Publishing Company, 2014.

Sarcone, Gianni A., and Marie-Jo Waeber. *Optical Illusions: An Eye-Popping Extravaganza of Visual Tricks.* Mineola, NY: Dover Publications, 2014.

WEBSITES

nei.nih.gov/kids/optical_illusions
This National Eye Institute page has information on optical illusions and a video to watch.

www.optics4kids.org/illusions
This web page explores 17 optical illusions with a quiz.

Publisher's note to educators and parents: Our editors have carefully reviewed these websites to ensure that they are suitable for students. Many websites change frequently, however, and we cannot guarantee that a site's future contents will continue to meet our high standards of quality and educational value. Be advised that students should be closely supervised whenever they access the Internet.

INDEX